An Introduction to
British Birds
A Photographic Guide

Nick Williams
Edited by Dereen Taylor

WAYLAND

This book is a differentiated text version of
The Wayland Book of Common British Birds by Nick Williams

First published in Great Britain in 2009 by Wayland,
a division of Hachette Children's Books

Wayland
338 Euston Road,
London NW1 3BH

Editor: Julia Adams
Designer: Ruth Cowan
Photographer: Nick Williams

Cover photograph: Mute swan
Title page: A robin feeding its young.
This page (from top): A song thrush in winter; a blue tit feeding its young; a greyling goose with chicks; young grey herons.
Contents page (from top): A male greenfinch; a juvenile great spotted woodpecker;
a male blackbird; a long tailed tit feeding its young.
Artwork on page 44 supplied by Nick Hawken.

British Library Cataloguing in Publication Data
Williams, Nick, 1948-
   An introduction to British birds
   1. Birds - Great Britain - Juvenile literature 2. Birds -
Great Britain - Identification - Juvenile literature
   I. Title II. Taylor, Dereen
   598'.0941

ISBN 978 0 7502 5438 0

Printed and bound in China

Wayland is a division of Hachette Chidren's Books, an Hachette Livre
UK company

www.hachettelivre.co.uk

Contents

Introduction

There are about 8,650 species of birds in the world. About 500 of these have been seen in Britain. However, only about 250 species are seen in Britain regularly. In fact, more than 100 species have been seen here by birdwatchers less than ten times.

This book includes 50 common British birds. All of them can be seen in gardens, parks, while out walking or driving.

The birds you see will depend on where you live. House sparrows and blackbirds are part of daily life in towns and the countryside. Birds like the great spotted woodpeckers are fewer in number. They are more often seen in large gardens, parks and woodlands.

Some birds, such as swallows and house martins, are only seen in Britain during the summer. These birds eat insects and they migrate south to Africa in winter to find food.

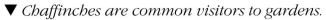

▼ *Chaffinches are common visitors to gardens.*

▲ *Spotted flycatchers migrate to Britain for the summer.*

◀ Mute swans can be found on ponds, lakes and rivers all over Britain.

▼ Robins sing throughout the year.

There are many ways to identify birds. Their shape, size, colour and the things they do all give important clues. Many birds also sing, and it is useful to learn their songs.

Why not keep a birdwatcher's notebook? You can write down the species, number, eating habits and songs of the birds you see. You could even make quick sketches of them.

▶ Black-headed gulls in winter plumage. They can be seen inland as well as on the coast.

House sparrow

Latin name: *Passer domesticus*

Size: 14.5 cm

Family: sparrows

Habitat: towns and cities, farms

The house sparrow is probably the best-known small bird in Britain. The male has a grey head and black front. Its brown back is streaked with black and it has a white bar on its wings.

Females and young are a mixture of paler browns and greys.

House sparrows like to make their nests hidden away in buildings. They also nest in holes in trees and in nest boxes. They normally have three broods in a year.

House sparrows will eat most things put out for them on a bird table. But during the breeding season, they eat mainly insects. They can often be seen in large flocks.

▲ *The male house sparrow has attractive grey, black and brown feathers.*

◄ *The female bird is much plainer than the male.*

Starling

Latin name: *Sturnus vulgaris*

Size: 21.5 cm

Family: starlings

Habitat: towns and cities, farms

Starlings live in large flocks and can make a lot of noise and mess. They make untidy nests out of straw in holes in buildings or trees. This makes them unpopular with some people.

Starlings may look like blackbirds but they are smaller and their wings are more pointed.

Although they look black, starlings' plumage actually has a beautiful green or purple sheen. They have yellow beaks.

Starlings will eat almost anything, but suet and cheese are favourite foods. Starlings are, in fact, good for gardens. They eat the larvae of craneflies, or 'daddy-long-legs' and other grubs that eat plants.

▶ *In summer, starlings have a green or purple sheen to their plumage.*

◀ *In winter, starlings have white tips on their feathers that look like spots.*

Blackbird

Latin name: *Turdus merula*

Size: 25 cm

Family: thrushes

Habitat: woodlands and gardens

The male blackbird is black all over. The females and young are brown with darker spots on their breasts.

Blackbirds usually build nests in bushes and hedgerows. The nest is a cup shape and is made of grasses held together with mud.

Blackbirds lay up to three clutches of eggs a year. The young are fed on mostly worms by their parents. Adult birds also eat insects, fruits and berries.

The male blackbird has a beautiful song. It sings all through the breeding season.

▲ *A young blackbird. Mum and dad will feed it for another two or three weeks.*

◀ *A male blackbird has a yellow beak and a yellow ring around its eyes.*

Robin

Latin name: *Erithacus rubecula*

Size: 14 cm

Family: thrushes

Habitat: woods, parks and gardens

The robin, or 'robin redbreast', is Britain's national bird. Its famous front is actually orange, not red. Males and females look alike. The young have a dark brown, speckled plumage.

Robins sing a beautiful song all year round. They guard their territory and fight off other robins if they come too near to their nests.

Robins start breeding in mid-April. They have two or three broods in a year. Their nests are made out of dead leaves, moss and grass.

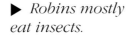 ▶ *Robins mostly eat insects.*

◀ *Robin nests are usually well-hidden. This one is on the ground, sheltered by leaves and grass.*

Song thrush

Latin name: *Turdus philomelos*

Size: 23 cm

Family: thrushes

Habitat: edge of woodlands, parks, gardens

▼ *Male and female song thrushes look the same.*

▶ *Mistle thrushes are larger than song thrushes, and not as common.*

Song thrushes have plain brown backs and very pale orange breasts covered in black spots. When they fly, they show orange 'arm-pits' underneath their wings.

The song thrush nests on the edges of woodlands and in parks and gardens. It lines its nest with mud, and lays blue eggs with black spots on them.

Like all thrushes, the song thrush loves to sing. It will often sing until after dark.

Song thrushes eat worms, slugs, insects, fruit and berries. They can also crack open snails by holding the snail's shell in their beak and smashing it against a stone.

Wren

Latin name: *Troglodytes troglodytes*

Size: 9.5 cm

Family: wrens

Habitat: woodlands, farmland and gardens

In very cold weather a group of wrens may roost together in one nest box to keep warm. Sixty-one have been found in one box!

The tiny wren is one of the most common birds in Britain. It will live anywhere it can find a place to hide. It likes to search for insect larvae and spiders instead of visiting bird tables.

The wren is easy to recognise by its small size and cocked tail. However, it is more likely to be heard than seen. It has a very loud voice for such a small bird. But the wren is not Britain's smallest bird. Goldcrests and firecrests are smaller at only 9 cm.

Wrens like to nest in old tree trunks covered in ivy. The male birds makes several nests. The female then chooses one of them to nest in.

▲ *This wren has used an old swallow's nest to lay its eggs in.*

▼ *You can tell a wren by its cocked tail.*

Great tit

Latin name: *Parus major*

Size: 14 cm

Family: tits

Habitat: woodlands, fields and gardens

The great tit is the largest member of the tit family. It has a green back, black and white head, and a black stripe down its yellow breast. The male bird has a much broader black stripe than the female.

All tits are very acrobatic birds. The great tit uses its agility to find insects, insect larvae, spiders, slugs and plant buds to eat.

Its large size means the great tit can crack open acorns. It holds the nut in its feet and hammers at it with its beak.

Like all tits, great tits lay only one clutch of eggs a year. This clutch can have 12 or 13 eggs in it. The eggs hatch in May.

▲ *Young chicks in a nest box.*

▼ *A male great tit. The female has a thinner black stripe on its breast.*

Blue tit

Latin name: *Parus caeruleus*

Size: 11.5 cm

Family: tits

Habitat: originally woodland, now urban

The blue tit is the best-known member of the tit family. Its crown, wings and tail are blue.

The blue tit is a popular garden bird and it often uses nest boxes and bird tables. It can be seen hanging upside-down from bird tables.

Blue tits lay the first of their eggs in early May. The young hatch after about two weeks. They are fed small green moth caterpillars by both parents.

Out of 12 young blue tits only one may get to breed the following year. This is because predators, such as cats, kill young blue tits.

▲ *This young blue tit has just grown feathers.*

◄ *Sunflower seeds are a favourite food of the blue tit.*

Coal tit

Latin name: *Parus ater*

Size: 11.5 cm

Family: tits

Habitat: parks, gardens, conifer woods

The coal tit has a black crown, white cheeks, brown back and grey belly. It has a white patch on the back of its head.

The coal tit is unusual because it likes to live among conifer trees. It usually nests close to the ground, or even under ground, at the base of a tree. It also likes to nest in old stone walls.

The coal tit also visits garden bird tables. It likes to eat cone seeds.

▲ *Coal tits have a white patch on the back of their heads.*

Coal tits take nuts and store them. But they do not always remember where they have put them!

▼ *Coal tits like to live among conifer trees.*

Dunnock

Latin name: *Prunella modularis*

Size: 14.5 cm

Family: accentors

Habitat: woodland, farmland, parks and gardens

The dunnock is a very common British bird. It is often called the hedge sparrow, although it is not related to the sparrow family. It has a blue-grey head and breast, a brown back and wings with dark streaks. Males and females look alike.

Dunnocks creep around under hedgerows looking for insects and small worms to eat.

▼ *Some people think dunnocks look like house sparrows.*

They usually only visit bird tables when other birds are not around.

The dunnock lays four or five blue eggs in its neat nest. It has two or three broods a year.

The dunnock's musical song is a common sound in the spring and summer.

▼ *Dunnocks line their nests with moss.*

Chaffinch

Latin name:	*Fringilla coelebs*
Size: 15 cm	
Family: finches	
Habitat: woodland, parks and gardens	

▲ *The male chaffinch is one of the most colourful British birds.*

▼ *The female chaffinch is much paler than the male.*

The male chaffinch is a beautiful bird. It has a reddish body and grey head. When it flies, you can see white bars on its wings and white feathers on the outside of its tail. The female is mainly pale brown and grey.

During the winter, chaffinches often group together in large flocks in the open countryside and on the edges of woodland, where they search for seeds to eat.

Chaffinches have a distinctive 'pink-pink' call. Their neat nests are made of grasses, mosses, spiders' webs, feathers and hair.

Greenfinch

Latin name: *Carduelis chloris*

Size: 14.5 cm

Family: finches

Habitat: farmland, parks and gardens

The male greenfinch's plumage is yellow and green with bits of grey. Its forked tail has a dark tip. The female is slightly browner and looks like a female house sparrow.

Greenfinches like to visit bird tables. They will fight other birds for food. They eat mainly seeds and love sunflower seeds. Peanuts from feeders are important in late winter and early spring when other food can be hard to find.

Greenfinches nest in bushes, hedgerows and sometimes trees.

The male greenfinch has a twittering song that is often followed by a wheezing sound.

▲ *A male greenfinch.*

▼ *The female greenfinch has yellow patches on its wings.*

Collared dove

▲ *A pair of collared doves.*

◄ *Collared doves often perch on posts and television aerials.*

Latin name: *Streptopelia decaocto*

Size: 32 cm

Family: pigeons and doves

Habitat: towns and farmland

Doves and pigeons pick up grit from the roadside. The grit helps them to grind up their food.

The collared dove came to Britain from the Balkan area of Eastern Europe in 1955.

Nowadays, the collared dove is a very common sight. It can often be seen sitting on telephone wires. It makes a 'coo-cooo-coo' call. The middle note of the call is longer than the other two.

Collared doves eat grain. If they can find enough food they will breed throughout the year. Normally, they have two or three broods a year.

Like most doves and pigeons, collared doves make a flat nest out of twigs. They lay two white eggs. They like to nest in conifer trees and often nest close to houses.

Wood pigeon

Latin name: *Columba palumbus*

Size: 41 cm

Family: pigeons and doves

Habitat: fields, woods, parks and gardens

Feral pigeons live in towns. They are smaller than wood pigeons and usually darker.

▶ *The wood pigeon has white patches on its neck.*

◀ *Feral pigeons are found in most towns and cities.*

The wood pigeon is the largest of the pigeons. It is grey and has two white bars on its wings. These are easier to see when it is flying. It also has white patches on the sides of its neck.

Wood pigeons can be seen in huge flocks. Farmers don't like them because they eat their crops.

In parks and large gardens, wood pigeons can become quite tame. However, if they are disturbed in the countryside, their wings make a clapping noise as they suddenly fly off.

Thousands of wood pigeons are shot every year, but they are still very common.

Great spotted woodpecker

Latin name:	*Dendrocopos major*
Size:	23 cm
Family:	wrynecks and woodpeckers
Habitat:	woodlands, parks, large gardens

The great spotted woodpecker is black and white. It has a red patch under its tail. The male also has a small red patch on the back of its head.

Like all woodpeckers, it has two toes facing backwards and two toes facing forwards.

This means it can cling on to the trunks of trees. It then drills into the bark with its beak, looking for insects.

During the breeding season, it uses its powerful beak to make large holes in nest boxes. This is so it can get inside and eat the eggs or young of other birds. It also feeds on seeds and nuts.

Great spotted woodpeckers drill a new hole in a tree trunk to nest every year.

▼ *This male great spotted woodpecker is using its tail to keep its balance.*

▼ *Young birds have red heads.*

Pied wagtail

▲ *Six newly-hatched pied wagtail chicks.*

Latin name: *Motacilla alba*

Size: 18 cm

Family: wagtails

Habitat: fields and parks, town centres

The pied wagtail can be found anywhere except in woodlands and on high mountains. It is often seen in school fields and parks.

Pied wagtails are grey and white birds. The male is darker than the female.

They have an unusual way of walking and running. As they search for insects to eat, they bob their heads up and down and wag their tails. Pied wagtails nest in sheltered holes in buildings or rock faces. Their call is a sharp 'chizzick' sound, which they make when they are flying.

▲ *The pied wagtail can often be seen in parks in Britain.*

21

Magpie

Latin name: *Pica pica*

Size: 46 cm

Family: crows

Habitat: fields, parks and gardens

The magpie has black and white plumage and a long tail. Like all crows, magpies are clever and adaptable birds.

The magpie's nest is made of sticks and wood. It is lined with roots and wool, and has a domed roof. Magpies eat many different things, including the eggs and young of other birds.

Magpies are normally seen alone. When they are not breeding, they sometimes gather in noisy, chattering groups.

▲ *A young magpie. The last part of any bird to grow is its tail feathers.*

◄ *A magpie sitting on a fence post.*

22

Jackdaw

Latin name: *Corvus monedula*

Size: 33 cm

Family: crows

Habitat: fields, woods, parks and gardens

The jackdaw is the smallest crow commonly seen in Britain. It looks black all over, but has a grey neck and cheeks.

Jackdaws normally live in open countryside. They nest in groups called colonies and build their nests in holes in trees and cliffs. During the winter jackdaws often join rooks to make large flocks. Sometimes hundreds of birds search for worms and grubs in open fields.

Jackdaws use bird tables and will even search rubbish bins for food.

Jackdaws are also seen in towns. They often nest in chimneys and churches. Their loud 'jack' call can be heard from far away.

▲ *Jackdaws have silvery-blue eyes.*

◄ *A young jackdaw.*

Rook and carrion crow

Latin name: *Corvus frugilegus* and *Corvus corone cornix*

Size: about 46 cm

Family: crows

Habitat: rook – fields, carrion; crow – everywhere, including cities and woodlands

Rooks and carrion crows are about the same size, and look black all over. The rook actually has a grey-white face and throat. Carrion crows are usually seen alone or in pairs. Rooks are nearly always in groups.

A rook's nesting site is called a rookery. It is built high up in tree branches and can be made up of more than a hundred nests. The carrion crow nests alone.

The carrion crow eats carrion, which is the flesh of dead animals. It also eats worms, insects, plants, rubbish and the eggs of other birds. Rooks eat plants, insects, larvae and worms.

Scotland has hooded crows instead of carrion crows.

◀ *Young rooks that have just hatched.*

▼ *The rook has a paler, thinner beak than the carrion crow.*

▼ *The carrion crow has a black body and beak.*

Black-headed gull

Latin name: *Larus ridibundus*

Size: 36 cm

Family: gulls

Habitat: inland, countryside

The black-headed gull is the smallest British gull. It is the gull most often found inland. It is seen in fields as they are being ploughed. It follows the farmer's tractor and eats worms and larvae in the soil. It is also found on playing fields and rubbish dumps.

The adult's head is actually dark brown during the breeding season (from March to August). In early autumn it loses its dark feathers and white ones grow. A small spot of darker feathers is left behind each eye.

Like all gulls, black-headed gulls breed in colonies.

▲ *During the breeding season, black-headed gulls have dark heads.*

▼ *An adult in winter plumage.*

▶ *This common gull looks similar to a black-headed gull in winter.*

Herring gull

Latin name: *Larus argentatus*

Size: 55–60 cm

Family: gulls

Habitat: coasts, seaside towns

▲ *The herring gull is the most commonly seen gull by the coast.*

▶ *Herring gulls have dark wing tips.*

The herring gull is the gull you are most likely to see around the coast of Britain. Common gulls (see photograph on page 25) are much smaller and found in Scotland.

Herring gulls nest on cliffs. They also nest among the chimneys of seaside houses. Their loud morning calls can often be heard in seaside resorts.

Herring gulls eat anything they can find and are a common sight in harbours and rubbish tips. They also eat the eggs and young of other birds, even other herring gulls.

▼ *Two young herring gulls getting ready to fly for the first time.*

Mute swan

Latin name: *Cygnus olor*

Size: 152 cm

Family: swans, ducks and geese

Habitat: water

Mute swans are one of the heaviest
flying birds in the world.
One weighed 25 kg and was
too heavy to take off!

Mute swans are very large, graceful birds. They are found on ponds, rivers, lakes and even coastal waters. They are normally seen in pairs. Young birds sometimes gather in large groups.

Mute swans normally start breeding when they are three years old. They usually stay with the mate they breed with for life. They build a nest in April.

Young swans are called cygnets. They have soft grey down when they hatch. Cygnets are looked after by both the male (the cob) and the female (the pen).

Swans eat water plants and graze on grassy river banks.

◀ *When cygnets have brown, untidy feathers they are sometimes called 'ugly ducklings'.*

▼ *Mute swans have long, strong necks.*

Mallard

Latin name: *Anas platyrhynchos*

Size: 58 cm

Family: swans, ducks and geese

Habitat: water

The mallard is the most common type of duck in Britain. Almost every pond and river running through a town or city has mallards on it.

The male is called the drake. It is more colourful than the female, which is brown all over. The female mallard needs to be camouflaged while it sits on its clutch of up to 12 eggs. Foxes, stoats and crows are all a threat, because they eat mallard eggs and ducklings.

Mallards normally eat water plants, grasses, seeds and insects.

▲ *The male mallard has a green head.*

◀ *This female mallard is watching over her two ducklings.*

Moorhen

Latin name: *Gallinula chloropus*

Size: 33 cm

Family: rails

Habitat: water

▲ *Moorhens have yellow feet and a white patch under the tail.*

▲ *Moorhen chicks may leave the nest for a short time a couple of hours after hatching.*

The moorhen is found on ponds, lakes, rivers and canals. As it swims, it jerks its head backwards and forwards.

Moorhens look almost black but they actually have a brown back and wings. Their beaks are red with a yellow tip.

Moorhens spend a lot of time out of the water running around searching for food. They eat plants, worms and insects.

Their very long toes help them to walk across floating plants such as lily pads.

Moorhens nest on the ground in plants near the water's edge or in branches overhanging the water. They have two or sometimes three broods a year.

Coot

Latin name: *Fulica atra*

Size: 38 cm

Family: rails

Habitat: water

▲ *Both male and female coots look the same.*

▲ *A mother with new chicks. Can you see their bald heads?*

Coots are the only British birds with pure white beaks.

Coots are closely related to moorhens. The two birds can often be seen together, but coots prefer to live on larger patches of water. In winter, as many as 5,000 coots can group together in a flock.

Coots are black all over, with a white beak. They have round parts on each toe to help them swim more easily.

They build their nests among plants and trees near the water's edge. The young hatch after about three weeks. They are able to swim and walk a few hours after hatching.

Young coots have a bright pink bald head. This might be where the saying 'as bald as a coot' comes from.

Canada goose

Latin name: *Branta canadensis*

Size: about 100 cm

Family: swans, ducks and geese

Habitat: water

Canada geese were brought to Britain from North America about 300 years ago. Those living in North America migrate but those living in Europe usually do not.

They are large brown birds with black necks and heads. They have white cheek patches that go under their heads.

Canada geese can be found on large lakes, rivers and sometimes on smaller stretches of water. They normally live together in colonies. They become very aggressive and make a hissing noise if their nests are approached.

The young are called goslings. They can fly at around nine weeks. Goslings stay with their parents for their first winter.

▲ *Canada geese are often seen in small flocks.*

◀ *Another kind of goose is the greylag goose.*

Grey heron

Latin name: *Ardea cinerea*

Size: about 95 cm

Family: bitterns and herons

Habitat: water

▲ *Herons can stand very still for a long time.*

▲ *Grey herons are always very alert.*

Grey herons are large, grey and white birds with black streaks. They have long beaks that look like daggers. They can be seen standing still or slowly walking in shallow water. As they fly they can make a 'fraank' call.

Grey herons eat fish, frogs, insects and small mammals. During the breeding season they also eat the young of other water birds.

Mostly, grey herons are seen on their own. They breed in colonies. These can be made up of more than 100 nests. Their large nests are built up in trees. Grey herons can live for 20 years.

Pheasant

Latin name: *Phasianus colchicus*

Size: male 76–89 cm; female 53–63 cm

Family: partridges, quails, pheasants

Habitat: open countryside near woodland

Pheasants are normally seen on the ground. They roost in trees so that foxes cannot catch them while they are asleep.

The Romans may have brought pheasants to Britain about 2,000 years ago. Pheasants are game and are often bred for shooting.

The male is usually a brown and gold colour, with a dark green face. It has a red eye wattle and a very long tail. Some males have a white ring round the neck.

The females do not have such long tails. They are a lighter brown all over. This camouflages them from predators when they are sitting on their eggs.

The nest is always well hidden on the ground. A male pheasant may have a number of mates sitting on eggs at the same time.

▲ *Male pheasants have red wattles around their eyes.*

◄ *The male pheasant often stands guard over the female.*

33

Kestrel

Latin name: *Falco tinnunculus*

Size: 34 cm

Family: falcons

Habitat: all over, except woodlands

The most common falcon in Britain is the kestrel. They can be seen more often than any other bird of prey. Kestrels are often seen hunting on the edges of motorways. They eat the small mammals, insects and birds that live there in shrubs and trees.

Kestrels hunt their prey by watching and waiting. They sit on a telephone wire or branch and wait. The kestrel can also hover for a long time. It moves its wings and tail very slightly so it can keep its eyes fixed firmly on one spot.

The nests of kestrels are usually found in holes in trees, old buildings or cliff ledges.

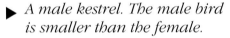

▶ *A male kestrel. The male bird is smaller than the female.*

▶ *These young kestrels are about one month old. They are almost ready to fly.*

34

Buzzard

Latin name: *Buteo buteo*

Size: 55 cm

Family: hawks, vultures and eagles

Habitat: fields and woodland

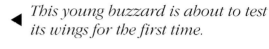

◄ *This young buzzard is about to test its wings for the first time.*

▲ *Some buzzards have light brown speckled feathers.*

Buzzards have become common all over the British countryside during the last ten years. They often sit on posts near to the roadside.

Buzzards often fly over woods, which is also where they nest. They are birds of prey, and eat mice, young rabbits and other small animals.

Birds that look like a buzzards and have a forked tail are called red kites.

Some buzzards are light brown, – others are quite dark.

Swallow

Latin name: *Hirundo rustica*

Size: 19 cm

Family: swallows and martins

Habitat: open fields, near water and quiet farm buildings

British swallows migrate every winter to southern and central Africa. They fly back again in the spring to breed. The journey in one direction can be as long as 8,000 km.

Swallows have a dark blue back, reddish forehead and deeply-forked tail. Males have long tail feathers called streamers. The females have shorter streamers.

The nest of a swallow is made of mud and grass. It is lined with feathers. It is often built up on a ledge inside a farm shed or garage.

At the end of the summer young swallows join the adult birds on their journey back to Africa.

▲ *A male swallow showing its long streamers.*

▼ *These young swallows are nearly ready to leave the nest. They are almost three weeks old.*

House martin

Latin name: *Delichon urbica*

Size: 12.5 cm

Family: swallows and martins

Habitat: towns and cities

The house martin is related to the swallow. It looks black, but is actually a very dark blue. It has white under-parts and a white patch on its bottom. Its forked tail does not have streamers like the swallow's tail.

House martins migrate and spend the winter in Africa.

Before humans built houses, house martins nested on cliffs. Now they live in towns and cities, as long as the air is not too polluted, because this kills the insects they eat.

House martins build their nests on the outsides of buildings. The nest is completely covered up, with just a small hole for getting in and out.

▲ *Can you see what insect this house martin is feeding its chicks?*

◄ *A house martin collecting mud for its nest.*

Sixteen other common birds

Fieldfare – 27 cm

The fieldfare is a type of thrush. It likes to eat apples and berries. Fieldfares are visitors to Britain.

Tree sparrow – 14 cm

The tree sparrow is similar to a house sparrow, but less common. It has a reddish-brown cap on its head and white cheeks with a black spot on them.

Long-tailed tit – 14 cm

The long-tailed tit is a common bird along woodland edges. The tail is more than half the bird's total length.

Redshank – 27 cm

Redshanks are wading birds. They are found on marshes and meadows near water. They have an orange-red beak and legs, and a brown back.

Green woodpecker – 32 cm

Green woodpeckers spend a lot of their time on the ground looking for ants. Males and females are yellowy-green with red heads.

Goldfinch – 12 cm

Goldfinches get their name from the golden wing bars which can be seen when they fly. Goldfinches are often seen in groups, called 'charms'.

Spotted flycatcher – 14 cm

The spotted flycatcher only visits Britain for about four months in the summer. It is not very common anymore, but you may see one in a park or garden.

Nuthatch – 14 cm

Nuthatches have a black stripe through the eye. They are good climbers and can walk head first down tree trunks. They like nuts.

Tawny owl – 38 cm

If you hear an owl hooting, it is likely to be a tawny owl. You probably won't see one, though, as they are nocturnal. This means they only come out at night.

Oystercatcher – 43 cm

Oystercatchers mainly live near coastal waters. They have black and white wings. They use their long, orange beaks to find worms, crabs and mussels. They don't often eat oysters!

Yellowhammer – 17 cm

Yellowhammers have a bright yellow head. They are seen all year round in fields and hedgerows. The sound of their song is often written down as 'a little bit of bread and no cheese'.

Sparrowhawk – 30–38 cm

Sparrowhawks are birds of prey. They mainly live in woodland. In cold weather they will visit gardens to try and snatch a bird from a bird table. They fly quickly and do not hover like kestrels.

Barn owl – 35 cm

This is the owl you are most likely to see. Barn owls often hunt in the evening or early morning. Their face and body feathers are white.

Jay – 34 cm

The jay is the most colourful member of the crow family. It has a pinkish-brown body and blue and black wings. Jays love acorns and store hundreds of them to eat in winter.

Tufted duck – 43 cm

This is the most common duck in Britain after the Mallard. The male is black and white and the female is dark brown. They are often seen on deep park ponds.

Great crested grebe – 48 cm

Great crested grebes are often seen on lakes and canals. They used to be hunted for their head feathers, which were used to decorate hats.

Attracting birds to your garden

The best way to get birds to visit your garden or school grounds is to offer them food, water, nest boxes and shelter.

Putting out food is most important when the weather is cold. If you start, it is important that you carry on. This is because birds start to rely on the extra food and may travel from far away to get to it.

If you want to feed birds all year round, only put out foods during the breeding season that the birds would find for themselves. These include seeds and mealworms.

During the rest of the year, try to put out a wide range of foods. Potatoes, cheese, bacon rind, cereals and bread are all good. Always soak bread first, as it may swell in a bird's stomach. Never put out salted peanuts.

Collect nuts, berries and fruit fallen from trees in the autumn. You can save them and put them out in the winter. You can also buy wild bird food and seeds from pet shops.

▲ *A great spotted woodpecker feeding from a hanging feeder filled with peanuts.*

▼ *A blackbird making a meal out of an apple.*

▲ *A great tit eats suet bird cake from a coconut shell.*

▶ *Be wary of cats who will attack birds visiting your garden.*

Birds need to replace lost fat in their bodies in winter. Suet is a useful food and can be put out in grain form. It can also be used to make a bird cake. Add nuts and seeds to the melted suet. Pour it into a half coconut shell or margarine tub and let it set. Hang it upside down outside for the birds to visit.

You can grow plants in your garden that will attract birds. Choose plants that have lots of nuts, berries and seeds or those that insects like. Here are some examples: sunflower, poppy, holly, rowan and honeysuckle. Leaving an area of your garden to grow wild is also a good idea.

Bird tables can be hung from a branch of a tree, put on a pole or attached to a windowsill if you do not have a garden.

Hanging feeders are popular with some birds. Others prefer to feed on the ground, but be careful cats don't attack them.

Making a nest box

You will need a plank of wood 150 cm long, 15 cm wide and 2 cm thick.

Saw the plank into pieces for the back, base, roof, front and two sides, following the measurements on the diagram below.

Cut a circle in the front for the entrance hole, 17.5 cm from the bottom. A hole 2.8 cm wide will allow blue tits and tree sparrows to enter. House sparrows need a hole 3.8 cm wide. Starlings need a larger box and an entrance hole at least 4.5 cm wide.

Make one or two small drainage holes in the base of the box.

Fix the joints with screws or nails. Attach the roof with a hinge and use hooks and eyes to hold it on either side.

Treat the box with organic exterior wood preservative. You can use roofing felt to cover the roof and hinge.

Some birds like open-fronted boxes. These can be made in the same way, but without the front panel. It helps to make the base bigger by 3 cm.

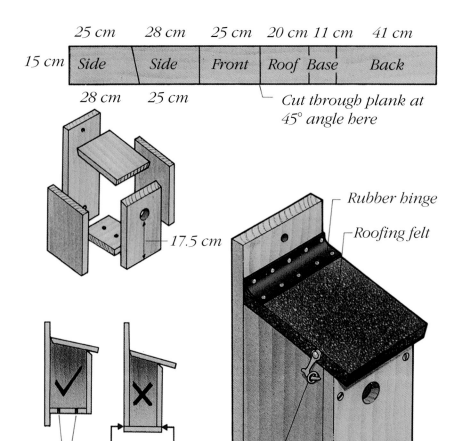

Small drainage holes

Water may enter here

Hook and eye

Rubber hinge

Roofing felt

17.5 cm

25 cm	28 cm	25 cm	20 cm	11 cm	41 cm
Side	Side	Front	Roof	Base	Back

15 cm

28 cm   25 cm

Cut through plank at 45° angle here

Here are some points to remember when putting up a nest box:

Children should not make a nest box without the help of an adult.

A new nest box should be put up by February.

Position the box so it is difficult for a cat to reach it.

Make sure the entrance hole does not face south into the Sun, or west into the rain.

Place the box so that the birds have a clear view of the garden from the entrance hole.

Do not put a perch under the hole. Predators may use it.

Make sure you can lift the lid off so that you can clean the box out in the autumn.

Bird surveys

Top 12 birds at my bird table:
1 House sparrow
2 Blackbird
3 Chaffinch
4 Collared dove
5 Greenfinch
6 Starling
7 Blue tit
8 Great tit
9 Dunnock
10 Robin
11 Song thrush
12 Coal tit

▲ *House sparrows and starlings at the bird table.*

This top 12 list counted the birds visiting one garden during January and February, 2008.

You can do your own survey. The birds will change depending on where you live, but most people will have a similar top 12, although maybe not in the same order.

The British Trust for Ornithology (BTO) is an organisation that surveys the number of wild birds in Britain. It asks volunteers to count the number of different birds that visit their garden. These surveys show which birds are most common in Britain, but also which ones are endangered.

In 2006, the BTO's survey showed that the most common bird in Britain was the chaffinch (14 million pairs). The blue tit was the next most common bird (11 million pairs), followed by the wood pidgeon and the blackbird (10 milion pairs each).

Glossary

Acrobatic Able to perform skilful and agile moves.

Aggressive Act in a threatening way.

Agility Quick-moving actions.

Bird of prey A bird that hunts and kills other animals for food.

Breeding season The time of year when birds and animals produce their young.

Camouflage Feathers or fur that blend in with scenery. Birds and animals use camouflage to hide from predators.

Conifer A tree, such as pine and fir, that has evergreen leaves and produces cones.

Clutch A number of eggs laid at one time.

Colonies Groups of birds that live and grow together.

Flocks Groups of birds that feed together.

Game Birds that are hunted by humans for sport and for food.

Habitat The place where a plant or animal naturally lives.

Identify To be able to work out what something is, for example to tell what species a bird belongs to.

Inland A part of the country that is not near the sea.

Larvae The young of some animals, particularly insects, that go through a complete change to become adults.

Mate One of a pair of birds.

Mealworm The larvae of the mealworm beetle.

Migrate To travel between two different places every year, spending the summer and winter seasons in different habitats.

Organic exterior wood preservative A special paint that protects and cares for wood that is exposed to the weather.

Pollution Dirty and unhealthy air and water. Pollution can be harmful to humans, animals and plants.

Plumage The feathers of a bird.

Predator An animal that hunts and kills other animals for food.

Roost To sleep or rest on a branch.

Sheen A gloss or shine on a surface.

Species A small group of animals or plants that are similar and can breed with each other.

Suet Raw beef or mutton fat.

Territory An area of land that an animal or pair of animals makes its own for breeding.

Wattle A loose fold of skin hanging from a bird's head or throat.

Woodland A large area of trees growing near each other.

Books to read

The Complete Illustrated Encyclopedia of British Birds by David Chandler and Russ Malin (Flame Tree Publishing, 2008)

Collins Complete Guide to British Birds: A Photographic Guide to Every Common Species by Paul Sterry (Collins, 2008)

RSPB Pocket Guide to British Birds by Simon Harrap (A & C Black, 2007)

British Birds Handbook by Duncan Brewer (Miles Kelley Publishing, 2006)

Other resources:

Birdwatching Magazine is available monthly at most large newsagents.

A Guide to British Garden Birds and Their Songs by Brett Westwood and Stephen Moss (BBC Audiobooks, 2008)

Birdwatcher's code

1 The birds always come first. Never disturb or frighten them. Try to keep away from their nests. Remember: it is against the law to take birds' eggs.

2 All types of habitat must be protected. Make sure you never damage habitats in any way. Don't drop any litter or pull out any plants.

3 Always ask permission before you go onto private land. Do not walk on crops or leave gates open.

Learn more about the wonderful world of wildlife

Wildlife Explorer is the junior section of The Royal Society for the Protection of Birds. The RSPB is Europe's largest wildlife conservation society. It fights to protect our wild birds and the countryside. The society also has over 100 nature reserves. When you join Wildlife Explorer, you will be able to visit these for free.

You can sign up to be a member of Wildlife Explorer on the RSPB's website: http://www.rspb.org.uk/youth/. As a member you get a membership pack with posters, stickers, a logbook with activities and a membership card. Members also receive a magazine six times a year and get to join in competitions.

Index

Page numbers in **bold** indicate pictures.